# BR BLUE
## THE NORTH IN FOCUS

STEPHEN OWENS

AMBERLEY

By the author of:

*BR Blue: A Personal Reflection*

First published 2021

Amberley Publishing
The Hill, Stroud
Gloucestershire, GL5 4EP

www.amberley-books.com

Copyright © Stephen Owens, 2021

The right of Stephen Owens to be identified as
the Author of this work has been asserted in
accordance with the Copyrights, Designs and
Patents Act 1988.

ISBN 978 1 3981 0714 4 (print)
ISBN 978 1 3981 0715 1 (ebook)

British Library Cataloguing in Publication Data.
A catalogue record for this book is available from
the British Library.

Typesetting by SJmagic DESIGN SERVICES, India.
Printed in the UK.

# Introduction

The photographs in this book were taken mostly in the northern half of the United Kingdom, in the period from 1978 to 1982. At this time the railway was still recognisably the one inherited from the steam age: quaintly old fashioned, caught in a time warp of its own making, old equipment going hand-in-hand with old working practices. The modern concepts of community rail and public service had not evolved, although closer examination may reveal that there were parts of the British Rail network operating in advance of these ideas – in Scotland, for example.

Not to be ignored, in keeping with the idea that the railway was being run on a shoestring, the rail fares were not overly expensive. Ticket prices were held at relatively low levels; by comparison they are much more costly today.

Because of this, it was not too surprising that an opportunity was recognised and the initiative seized to drag the railway into the future. This ambition has met with resistance at various levels and it remains unclear as to what the finished article will look like. Despite the uncertainty, in some places the transformation to the railway has been remarkable. Whether it has been worth all the upset is debatable and perhaps best left to future generations to judge. However, it would be churlish not to concede that the system today appears more modern, more efficient, and better integrated.

As I write this introduction, improvements are being made to the infrastructure at Entwistle station. Entwistle is about as remote as it is possible to get in densely populated industrial Lancashire. It lies just outside Greater Manchester. The station is to the south of Sough Tunnel, between Darwen and Bromley Cross; it is probably the highest point above sea level on the line from Blackburn to Bolton. The unmanned halt serves a tiny community and perhaps most famously a pub, but it remains a popular destination with hikers all year round. Over recent years the line has been continually downgraded. It was singled to reduce maintenance costs and mitigate a kink in the line through the tunnel, and later Entwistle became a request stop. The station appears somewhat forlorn – uncared for and all overgrown. There are no station buildings, as such, simply a rudimentary bus shelter-type waiting shed, which provides limited protection, if any, and the weather hereabouts can be pretty inclement.

When I passed through recently, I was surprised to see what was being done. Heavy machinery was in use and men in high-vis clothing were working on the project – clearly, serious money was being spent on improvements. Unusually, it wasn't raining, but nonetheless the whole scene appeared to be at odds with the green rural surroundings.

I recall that in the old days, when the line was still double track, Entwistle was an island platform, and in the 1970s, whenever the train I was on stopped at the station, no one ever seemed to get on or off. Incongruously, however, Entwistle had umpteen lengthy sidings to the north and east of the station – perhaps a little bit like Garsdale. Maybe the only thing I ever saw on these sidings was ballast hopper trucks. Be that as it may, I do remember being told that back in the day freight trains were often shunted into these to make way for passenger trains. At that time, in the 1960s, the line was quite busy and the climb to Entwistle for laden or empty coal trains was not something to be taken lightly, especially with the lengthy tunnel to negotiate.

When an opportunity presented itself I asked someone who I thought might know, what was going on at Entwistle. I was told that the platform was being rebuilt in preparation for the introduction of four-car units on the line. I asked if the track was being doubled, but my informant didn't know. There are places on the line where stretches of double track have been reinstated, and all the other stations on the line are designated passing places.

Regardless, I was impressed by the commitment to invest in the location. Although I thought it commercially difficult to justify unless new housing was planned for nearby, it seemed to illustrate perfectly a new ethos and enthusiasm for the railway. By the same token, I thought the need for all the expenditure such a waste. Had the line been properly maintained during its years of neglect, such an outlay wouldn't be necessary... but isn't that the story of the railway.

During the 1970s and 1980s the railway was largely ignored. The owners – the government – had other priorities and the railway would have to make do and mend.

Post privatisation in the mid-1990s, and after the introduction of the franchise system, the different operators simply focused on profit. It wasn't long before difficulties arrived and the ensuing consequences became impossible to ignore.

However, more recently, following the financial crash of 2008, there has been a change of emphasis. The coalition government of 2010 launched a new, different strategy: to revive the Northern Powerhouse.

There was a belief that in the north the infrastructure was inadequate. Because of this, the region was lagging behind in some way: economic growth had stalled and it could not fulfil its potential. Whether this was true or not is debateable. It was definitely not the case in an earlier era when new roads were being built and railway lines closed and stations shut. Was there ever a likelihood that any amount of investment in the infrastructure would bring back the industry that had gone?

Perhaps it could be suggested that the railway has been a casualty of muddled political thinking. The closures were a mistake. Earlier governments had no long-term plan for public transport. They were short-sighted, preferring to believe that immediate savings could be made by reducing the size of the network, by getting rid of the unprofitable subsidised lines. Today, events seem to have gone full circle. There is now a realisation that any investment in the rail infrastructure will have lasting economic benefits, and that this will result in improved connectivity and greater efficiency.

Undoubtedly, it is true that over recent years the economy of the north has changed considerably. It has become less fragmented and more centralised. Smaller towns have declined and become satellites of their nearby large, domineering cities. It seems that Liverpool, Manchester and Leeds all draw in people from further and further afield, from towns that once had industry and employment – factories, mills and mines.

While this has been a boon to the economies of the larger cites, the smaller towns have declined even further. Having lost their industry, they then lose their labour force, and their sustainability becomes questionable. Some of these towns have been incorporated into larger metropolitan authorities: Bolton, Bury and Stockport have become part of Greater Manchester, for example. Perhaps what has happened to the football teams in these towns is evidence of something more significant.

Both of my former home towns have fallen victim to these economics; both have declined, with manufacturing industry lost and not replaced. Inevitably, people have moved away – gone to live where there is work, or they commute to the cities where they have been able to get a job.

At one time both Keighley and Blackburn had busy goods yards. Obviously, they were not alone in this respect. In Keighley, on my way to school in a morning, I would often see steam loco from Lawkholme Lane Bridge shunting trucks. The yard in Blackburn was active into the 1980s and the coal depot was still open. Not today. Now the lack of jobs in these smaller towns has led to an increase in the number of people heading off each morning to Leeds or Manchester. Serious overloading and passenger discomfort on these commuter services has been widely reported. At the moment there seems to be no suggestion of investing in the smaller towns to ensure they can provide job opportunities and have an independent viability.

It seems to have been totally forgotten that even in the 1980s the Northern Powerhouse was just about still intact, even if the core industries were in decline. There was no initiative then to do anything for the north – quite the contrary. The home of dirty industry was seen as being in the developing world, and the new way forward for the developed world was the service sector. Globalisation meant specialisation, and if you worked in an industry that could not compete in an unequal world, you were finished.

From 1978 onwards, during the period often referred to as 'BR blue', I was able to photograph some of what I saw on the railway for posterity. Some might suggest that this was not a pretty sight; certainly nothing special. The period didn't have the interest of the steam era – how could it? At the same time, it was an era when the railway appeared neglected and threadbare; yes, it was being run on a shoestring, and it looked and felt like it.

Be that as it may, it had its devotees and supporters. People seemed to instinctively recognise that the situation couldn't and wouldn't last. In a way it was similar to the end of steam: the clock was ticking, but this time no one knew when it would stop, nor what would follow.

Some Inter-City express services had been upgraded: the West Coast Main Line was electrified and HSTs were being introduced on the East Coast Main Line. However, on the less glamorous parts of the network little had changed since the 1960s. DMUs were the backbone of local and cross-country services, and smaller diesel locos hauled longer distance passenger trains on secondary routes – Crewe to Cardiff, for example.

The trains themselves seemed to be relics of an earlier era. Partially because they were, but really because any new investment was miniscule and easily absorbed. Institutionalised thrift was the all-pervading philosophy. Despite this, some new locos were acquired: the Class 56s and Class 58s. The arrival of these powerful freight engines – to haul coal trains – displaced some Class 37s and 47s, and these were cascaded to work on the beleaguered passenger network. Some were reallocated to Scotland, to replace the heroic Class 26s and 27s on trains out of Glasgow Queen Street and Inverness. Remarkably, these locos had operated over these scenic but remote routes for twenty years, and huge credit must go to the people who were able to maintain and operate them in such adverse conditions.

Even during this period, large numbers of commuters travelled to the larger cities by train. Mail and parcels still travelled by train, as did the newspapers. It may be unkind to say so, but if the travellers' tales are to be believed, on some services the commuters were treated little better than the mail and parcels. During the rush hours many trains were overcrowded, but, at least in my recollection, cancellations were rare.

Undoubtedly, there has been a switch in emphasis on the railway; the priorities have changed. There are many more people in the UK today than there was in 1980, and inevitably more people travel by train. Public transport has become a political issue and not solely because of environmental concerns. The railway has become a people carrier and is now more often identified as being one. Moving freight is no longer the railway's primary function; people are probably the major cargo of the railway today – little mail or parcels, and few newspapers. However, the railway is still conflicted between long-distance and short-haul passenger services, and these trains compete for the same space on the same track.

Recently, much has been made of the financial investment being made in the railway. The people who know most about this are the rail passengers themselves. They are the ones who have been most inconvenienced.

To accommodate the work necessary to improve the rail infrastructure, the different agencies seem to have made a number of catastrophic decisions. Inevitably the rail passenger has been the loser: those who use the railway the most have been the ones who have suffered the most. Cancellations and delays have become commonplace and temporary station closures have made the headlines – King's Cross, Waterloo and Liverpool Lime Street.

It could be suggested that the railway has been over ambitious: it tried to do too much in a limited time. It could also be suggested that much of what has been done was unnecessary. But let's not be so hasty or uncharitable.

In the 1960s the Northern Powerhouse was a fully functioning entity, although no one really recognised it or appreciated it for what it was; it was simply taken for granted. However, the world had changed. The industries that had evolved in the north manufactured products to meet the demands of empire and markets overseas. 'Manchester Goods' were exported worldwide. However, by the mid-1960s the empire had gone; not only that, but other nations were competing in the same marketplace and were able to produce similar products more economically. The writing was on the wall, but, mixing my metaphors, the dye was cast. By the mid-1980s the industrial base of the UK had been decimated – Trafford Park, Manchester, a wasteland. It seems the manufacturers were inflexible and that self-sufficiency – producing for the domestic market – was never a viable option.

Globalisation led to the mass transhipment of containerised goods. You can see piles of these things stacked up to the south of Manchester Piccadilly, and they come from all over the world, delivering things that were once made in Trafford Park and the north.

To its credit, the railway moved quite seamlessly into the bulk freight transportation business. It's a pity it was not able to do the same with the passenger business. It appears that the new regime thought the system unfit for purpose: the rolling stock unsuitable, the track layout illogical, the signalling out of date, and most of the stations badly designed. Furthermore, the scheduling of services was archaic: the timetable resembled something from the past; north–south was satisfactorily catered for, just about, but there was a significant shortfall in commuter and east–west services.

Perhaps it is because of all this that there is today an affection for the railway as it was in 1980, despite all its flaws. I suspect the truth is that most people don't really care about the rolling stock as long as they get a seat, nor do they care about the track layout or signalling. I suspect most people actually liked their old-fashioned, cold and windy stations, and care little if their journey time is a few minutes shorter, as long as their train is punctual and never cancelled.

Alas, there is no going back. The only consolation is that the preserved railways do a pretty fine job of recreating the atmosphere of a happier, more passenger friendly time. The desire to build an efficient modern railway has led to the arrival of an unreliable, impersonal one. One that is far removed from the British Rail many knew and loved.

Most of the photographs included here were taken with Olympus cameras. The majority were taken using an OM-1, with a standard 50-mm lens. For some shots I used a 135-mm telephoto lens and, very occasionally, a 28-mm wide angle lens. The majority of the images have been scanned from Kodak C41 print film negatives; there were a few occasions when I used Fuji. Also included are a number of images that have been scanned from black-and-white print film (either Ilford or Kodak), and a tiny number that have been scanned from E6 transparencies.

All the locations featured are in the north of the country. An unfortunate consequence of this is that there are no Class 33s or 50s in the selection – my apologies for the omission. However, I make no apology for the location duplication. Different weather, light, time of year, and the different trains and locos provide sufficient variety for the images to be included. There are passenger trains, all manner of freight trains, light engines and locos on shed. Diesel locomotives dominate, although shots of electric locos and DMUs have been included.

With some of the photos there may be a lack of specific detail: the number of the loco or the roster it was working, or where a freight train was actually going. I'm aware that many railway enthusiasts are fastidious in this regard; however, I was never a particularly thorough note taker, and, almost forty years on, my memory is far from reliable. Despite this, it is fortunate that there is so much information available in the public domain, and the accessibility of this helps to compensate for my own failure to write things down at the time.

The order in which the photos are presented follows the Trans-Pennine corridor, from Liverpool to Manchester and then to Leeds, Sheffield, Doncaster and York. These cities were all significant industrial centres in the day, and it is hoped that the Northern Powerhouse project will provide the necessary impetus for them to reclaim their importance.

The next shots in the sequence lead from Keighley to Skipton, Settle Junction and Garsdale. I come from Keighley originally, therefore perhaps inevitably feel an attachment to the Settle–Carlisle line. Skipton was the first shed I visited. It had a scrap line and occasionally something special on shed – Britannias 70001 and 70040, and Clan 72006, were the most memorable locos I saw there.

I lived in Blackburn during the 1970s and '80s and this goes some way to explaining why it features so heavily in this collection. The stabling point was always interesting and the line to Preston scenic, especially between Cherry Tree and Pleasington.

Following Blackburn is Preston to Carlisle, featuring the electrified West Coast Main Line, and finally a selection of shots taken in Scotland.

Most loco classes are fairly represented, apart from those mentioned above and perhaps the 56s. There are plenty of 25s and 40s in Lancashire, 45s and 55s in Yorkshire, and lots of 26s and 27s in Scotland. The 26s were a personal favourite and really the only class I knew anything about. They were workmanlike and reliable, and seemed to me courageous and deserving of respect. The various modifications they received added to their character and made some of the locos unique.

It has been said that to write one book you need to have read hundreds. Paraphrasing this, it could be suggested that to take decent photos you need to have taken thousands – and learnt from your mistakes. Most of what I ever learnt about photography was gained taking photos of trains, and by making lots and lots of mistakes. Later, I would reapply some of this knowledge in taking photos of very different subject matter and in totally different locations. This helped me to realise that often the best photos are taken in places the photographer knows well, where it is possible to revisit the same spot to perfect the image.

These days, I've become much more forgiving and tolerant of imperfections in railway photographs – chimneys or signals sticking out of the top of locos, and shadows cast in the wrong place or people interfering in some way with the view. Once, someone who knew all about the commercial value of photos authoritatively said to me, 'If it is there it's there...', or words to that effect.

Today, the photographer is able to use computer technology to mask their own shortcomings and airbrush out their misfortunes. I concede that I've been able to use the same technology to do things to images I never thought possible. Fortunately, I never disposed of the negatives, even if I did throw away unsatisfactory prints.

There is no high art here, simply straight-forward imagery: portraits of locos and trains in the landscape. They illustrate some of what I saw and how I saw it... when I had 20/20 vision.

Class 40 loco No. 40134 at Liverpool Lime Street waiting to depart with a passenger train. I am reasonably certain I travelled on the train to Preston, but I have no recollection of where it was going – possibly Barrow.

Class 86 electric loco No. 86210 *City of Edinburgh* at Liverpool Lime Street between duties with another unidentified electric loco. The station clock must have been a popular place to rendezvous – I hope it still is.

Class 47 loco No. 47405 at Liverpool Lime Street departing after being released from the passenger train it brought into the station. The cramped nature of the station's approach made such manoeuvres problematic.

Class 47 loco No. 47585 *County of Cambridgeshire* at Liverpool Lime Street waiting to depart with a passenger train. It would appear that the loco had only recently been named.

Class 25 loco No. 25042 at Wigan Springs Branch MPD.

Class 25 loco No. 25297 at Wigan Springs Branch MPD.

Class 40 loco No. 40091 at Wigan Springs Branch MPD.

Class 40 loco No. 40126 at Wigan Springs Branch MPD.

Class 25 loco No. 25075 at Manchester Victoria. I never realised how much I liked Victoria until it wasn't there any more. Obviously, it is still there, after a fashion, but it's nothing like the station I first visited in the mid-1960s.

Class 45 Peak loco No. 45072 at Manchester Victoria on pilot duty being passed by an unidentified Class 47 hauling a freight train. This will be one of the later photos in this selection – perhaps taken in 1985.

Class 45/6 Peak loco arriving at Manchester Victoria in bright winter sunshine hauling a Liverpool to Newcastle passenger train.

Class 40 loco No. 40127 at Manchester Victoria in the through roads awaiting right of way hauling a passenger train.

*Above*: Class 40 loco No. 40076 at
Manchester Victoria hauling a parcels train
probably destined for Red Bank on an overcast
afternoon. The scene illustrates perfectly how
Victoria was at the time: with the longest
platform imaginable and a permanently
grey sky.

*Left*: Class 45/6 Peak loco at Manchester
Victoria hauling a parcels train.

Class 47 loco No. 47302 at Manchester Victoria hauling an oil train. Unusually, the train had been diverted through this platform rather than going through the centre roads.

Class 40 loco No. 40157 coming down the hill from Miles Platting to Manchester Victoria hauling an oil train.

Class 45 Peak loco No. 45069 approaches Manchester Victoria hauling a Newcastle to Liverpool passenger train.

Class 46 loco No. 46017 approaches Manchester Victoria hauling a Newcastle to Liverpool passenger train in August 1982.

Class 40 loco No. 40197 at Manchester Victoria hauling an oil train.

Class 25 loco No. 25097 at Manchester Victoria with an unidentified Class 47 in tow on a bright, sunny, but snowy day. It would appear the locos have come from Newton Heath depot. The DMU in the picture was not part of the same train.

Class 25 loco No. 25144 at Manchester Victoria hauling a passenger train on a freezing cold frosty day. The 25 has no train heating boiler so the passengers must have endured a chilly journey, possibly from Southport. The loco has been fitted with mini-snowploughs and is adorned with three overhead wires warning flashes.

Class 40 loco No. 40168 at Manchester Victoria hauling a passenger train in August 1982. The battle scar on the front would indicate that the loco has recently had repairs.

Class 56 loco No. 56116 at Manchester Victoria hauling a coal train destined for a northern powerhouse. This again is one of the later photos here, the livery of the 56 being a bit of a giveaway.

Class 25 loco No. 25260 at Manchester Piccadilly. I recall taking this photo specifically because it was the first shot I took with a new 28-mm lens that I'd just bought. I think it is fair to suggest that the loco is not in the best of condition, but the lens was a winner. I would later become quite attached to it, although not so much for railway photography.

Class 31 loco at Manchester Piccadilly waiting to depart with a passenger train. Here again, the loco does not appear to be in tip-top condition; I can't imagine it inspired too much confidence from passengers. It is possibly No. 31184.

Class 45 Peak loco No. 45113 at Manchester Piccadilly waiting to depart with a passenger train, which could well be the Harwich Boat Train.

Class 81 electric loco No. 81008 at Manchester Piccadilly waiting to depart hauling a passenger train – 8 or 18? I would have liked it to have been the palindrome, but I am almost certain it is No. 81008.

Class 85 electric loco No. 85016 at Manchester Piccadilly waiting to depart with a passenger train.

Class 86 electric loco No. 86241 *Glenfiddich* arriving into Manchester Piccadilly hauling a passenger train from the south.

Class 76 electric loco No. 76011 at Reddish MPD. These unique locos are much missed; they hauled freight trains on the now closed Penistone line long after the Manchester Piccadilly to Sheffield Victoria passenger service was withdrawn. Retrospectively, the closure appears ever more regrettable.

Class 47 loco approaching Leeds City from the west in the mid-1980s hauling a passenger train made up of six Mk 1 carriages.

Class 45 Peak loco No. 45103 at Leeds hauling a passenger train.

Class 45 Peak loco No. 45126 at Leeds hauling a passenger train.

Class 47 loco No. 47144 at Leeds – light engine.

Class 55 Deltic loco No. 55006 *Fife & Forfar Yeomanry* at Leeds having just arrived with a passenger train from King's Cross. The shot must have been taken in around 1979, just before Deltics were replaced by HSTs on the service to and from the capital.

Class 56 loco No. 56024 at Knottingley MPD. I was amused by the 'No Parking' sign in the photo – I guess this doesn't apply to the 56.

Class 45 Peak No. 45145 at Sheffield hauling a passenger train.

Class 47 loco No. 47466 arriving at Sheffield hauling a passenger train from the south.

Class 31 loco No. 31184 at Sheffield hauling a passenger train. This black-and-white, gloomy scene from the early 1980s looks perhaps even older. These days, it appears unusual to see a mixed train.

Class 47 loco No. 47164 at Doncaster hauling a passenger train.

Class 47 loco at Doncaster hauling a freight train. The 47 is a 47/3, most likely one of those allocated to Knottingley, which spent most of their time pulling these merry-go-round coal trains.

Class 55 Deltic loco No. 55004 *Queen's Own Highlander* hauling a southbound passenger train.

Class 20 loco No. 20026 stabled at Scunthorpe. The photo is one of the earliest in this collection – spring 1978. Delightfully, the loco is still in the original BR green livery. The location could, or should, be identified as Frodingham.

Class 20 loco No. 20029 stabled at Scunthorpe/Frodingham.

Class 31 loco No. 31111 at York, reversing on to a passenger train.

Class 37 loco at York hauling a southbound freight train.

Class 40 loco No. 40035 *Apapa* at York hauling a southbound passenger train.

Class 40 loco No. 40195 at York, stabled at the MPD.

Class 55 Deltic No. 55017 *The Durham Light Infantry* at York, heading for home, hauling a northbound passenger train.

Class 55 Deltic No. 55021 *Argyll & Sutherland Highlander* at York, light engine, awaiting duty and basking in the afternoon sunshine on the centre roads.

Class 55 Deltic No. 55004 *Queen's Own Highlander* at York, looking a shadow of its former self: bereft of nameplates, forlorn and withdrawn.

A pair of Class 37 locos at Middlesbrough hauling a freight train. The leading loco is No. 37198. Steel on Teesside was an essential ingredient of the Northern Powerhouse and the economy of the north-east.

A pair of Class 31 locos at Keighley hauling a freight train. The photo is taken from Lawkholme Lane Bridge looking north toward Skipton. The old steam shed would once have stood where the industrial plant is on the right. I would cross this bridge in the 1960s on my way to and from school. Occasionally, wonderful and memorable things were to be seen, one being a Class 25, then referred to as a 'Brush Type 2', piloting a 9F on the Hunslet tanks. Although not having the same impact, the pair of 31s hauling the cement train from Grassington were at least able to conjure memories of times past.

A solitary Class 25 loco on the stabling point, a former Western Region Class 123 DMU on a Leeds to Morecambe service, and Class 40 loco No. 40063 hauling a freight train. This evocative picture was taken on 18 September 1982 from the bridge we would cross in the 1960s on the way to Skipton shed. It is difficult to compare that time with the early 1980s, but nonetheless the scene offers plenty to interest and suggests what it was like back then – semaphore signals, water towers and decaying, disused platforms.

Class 31 loco Nos 31276 and 31112 at Skipton on the stabling point accompanied by two unidentified Class 25s and a Class 101 DMU in September 1982.Class 25 loco No. 25199 at

Class 25 loco No. 25199 at Skipton on the stabling point.

Class 47 loco No. 47443 arriving at Skipton hauling a northbound Nottingham to Glasgow passenger train. Despite the building work being done in the background the photo still seems to have more to do with the past than the future.

Class 47 loco just to the north of Skipton hauling a Glasgow to Nottingham passenger train. In the early 1980s the 47s became increasingly common on this service, displacing the Peaks and the occasional Class 40.

Class 40 loco at Hellifield hauling a northbound diverted West Coast Main Line passenger train. On a wet autumn Sunday, I'm not quite sure why this loco was on this train, nor why I was on the station trying to take photos. Regardless, the appalling conditions make for an interesting picture and illustrate the inexplicable, compelling fascination of the railway, which was having to make do and mend. Although the passengers would be deprived of train heating – and probably in places, because of the weather, deprived of their view – they would appreciate, I'm sure, that they were not deprived of their train.

In stark contrast to the previous shot, a Class 25 loco hauling a southbound cement train on a sunny evening.

Class 40 loco No. 40183 at Long Preston hauling a freight train. The working is the Heysham Moss to Haverton Hill tanks.

Class 47 loco passes through Settle Junction hauling a slow-moving, northbound freight train. The original Settle station was hereabouts, prior to the construction of the line to Carlisle.

Class 40 loco climbing away from Settle Junction hauling a northbound mixed-freight train – the *Long Drag* has begun in earnest.

Class 45 Peak No. 45133 hauling the afternoon Leeds to Carlisle passenger train. When this photo was taken a steam special was due, but the through trains between Nottingham and Glasgow had been replaced on the Settle–Carlisle by two trains a day each way operating from Leeds to Carlisle. A variety of locos were used on the service.

Class 31 loco at Settle Junction hauling the afternoon Carlisle to Leeds passenger train.

Class 45/1 Peak loco at Settle Junction hauling a Glasgow to Nottingham passenger train. Taken a little earlier than the previous photo.

Class 45/6 Peak loco at Settle Junction hauling a Glasgow to Nottingham passenger train.

Class 47 loco at Settle Junction hauling a southbound freight train on a big blue day in the summer of 1982.

Class 40 loco No. 40183 at Settle Junction hauling the Heysham Moss to Haverton Hill tanks.

Class 47 loco No. 47540 arrives at Settle hauling a southbound Glasgow to Nottingham passenger train.

Class 45/1 Peak loco at Blea Moor hauling a Glasgow to Nottingham passenger train. Even on a day when the weather is fair, this remote location appears bleak and unforgiving.

Meeting at Dandry Mire Viaduct. North and southbound expresses pass on a sunny spring evening at Garsdale. The train to Glasgow is being hauled by a Class 45/6 Peak loco, while the train to Nottingham by a Class 47.

Moments later the Class 47 seen in the previous picture loco approaches Garsdale station hauling a Glasgow to Nottingham passenger train.

Class 40 loco No. 40060 at Blackburn hauling a parcels train. The Red Bank vans was usually the last of the diverted West Coast Main Line trains to pass through Blackburn. Here, it is seen joining the East Lancashire Line at Daisyfield.

Class 37 loco at Blackburn hauling the Sheffield to Blackpool North summer Saturday-only passenger train.

Class 40 loco No. 40141 at Blackburn on the stabling point in August 1982.

Class 40 loco at Blackburn on an overcast day hauling a freight train. Not sure of the identity of the loco, but the telltale bolts on the side reveal it once carried a name. The gash on the front could indicate that it is No. 40010 *Empress of Britain*.

Former Haymarket-allocated Class 40 loco No. 40064 at Blackburn sitting pretty on the stabling point.

Class 40 loco No. 40162 at Blackburn on the stabling point.

Class 40 loco No. 40148 at Blackburn hauling a freight train.

Class 40 locos at Blackburn. The near loco was coming on to the stabling point, while the loco in the distance shuts vans.

Class 25 loco departing Blackburn with a rake of coal empties.

Class 104 DMU at Lower Darwen, Blackburn, passing the site of the old loco shed. The three-car Manchester set, with the white stripe, would be unusual on this Manchester to Blackburn service. The photo was taken in autumn 1982, by which time the line had been singled.

Class 45 Peak loco at Mill Hill, Blackburn, hauling the Sheffield to Blackpool summer Saturday-only passenger train.

Class 40 loco No. 40170 climbing away from Mill Hill hauling a short freight train.

Class 40 loco No. 40128 between Cherry Tree and Mill Hill, hauling a freight train toward Blackburn. A summer afternoon in Lancashire: flat light and abundant Rosebay Willowherb, with Cherry Tree station in the background.

Class 104 DMU at Cherry Tree, Blackburn, on a Colne to Preston service. The snow and the winter sunshine make for an attractive picture of something considered ordinary at the time.

Class 40 loco hauling a failed DMU at Cherry Tree. Despite the failure, the Colne to Preston service was operating and if I recall correctly was more or less on time.

Class 25 loco No. 25143 at Cherry Tree hauling Class 40 loco Nos 40092 and 192 in July 1982. Presumably, this was a balance working with the locos being returned to Wigan or Preston.

Class 40 loco No. 40092 is pictured again at Cherry Tree hauling a westbound freight train comprised mostly of coal empties.

Class 40 loco No. 40143 at Cherry Tree hauling a freight train of coal empties. This is the same working as the one that appears in the previous photo.

Class 40 loco No. 40196 at Cherry Tree heading off into the late afternoon sunshine with only a guards' van in tow.

Class 47 loco No. 47337 at Cherry Tree hauling a westbound freight train.

Class 47 loco No. 47438 at Cherry Tree hauling a diverted WCML passenger train toward Preston on a sunny autumn Sunday.

*Above*: Class 25 loco at Cherry Tree hauling a freight train. This permanent way train was a regular working, and it was invariably pulled by a Class 25.

*Right*: Class 120 Cross Country DMU at Cherry Tree on a Blackpool North to Leeds service in the early 1980s. At the time there was only one train a day each way operating the through service on this line. Recently, the service has been much improved and operates hourly.

Class 105 Cravens DMU at Cherry Tree on a Preston to Colne service.

Class 25 loco No. 25083 at Cherry Tree hauling a permanent way train toward Blackburn.

Class 25 loco at Cherry Tree hauling what appears to be two freight trains toward Blackburn in October 1982.

Class 37 loco nears Cherry Tree hauling an oil train toward Blackburn.

On a summer morning in 1982, Class 40 loco nears Cherry Tree hauling a maintenance train toward Blackburn.

Under a threatening sky, Class 40 loco No. 40064 nears Cherry Tree hauling an evening freight train toward Blackburn.

Class 40 loco nears Cherry Tree hauling a freight train toward Blackburn in August 1982.

Class 104 DMU between Pleasington and Cherry Tree crossing the River Darwen, heading toward Blackburn on a Preston to Colne service. Perhaps remarkably, this view remains very similar today. The photo was taken from the A674 at Feniscowles.

Class 47 loco nears Cherry Tree hauling a coal train toward Blackburn. This is one of the later photographs included here.

Class 45 Peak loco approaching Pleasington hauling the Sheffield to Blackpool summer Saturday-only passenger train.

Class 47 loco nears Pleasington hauling a diverted WCML passenger train toward Preston on a murky Sunday afternoon.

Class 40 loco at Pleasington hauling a freight train, probably heading for Warrington. The train includes an electric locomotive – possibly a Class 83.

Class 37 loco at Pleasington hauling the Blackpool to Sheffield summer Saturday-only passenger train.

Class 40 loco No. 40096 at Pleasington hauling the Blackpool to Sheffield summer Saturday-only passenger train.

Class 47 loco at Hoghton, Preston, hauling a diverted WCML passenger train toward Preston on a bright sunny Sunday afternoon.

Class 85 electric loco at Leyland, hauling a southbound passenger train of Mk 1 carriages.

Class 25 loco at Preston, light engine, heading on to the stabling point. This is one of the earlier photos included here – probably 1978.

Class 25 loco No. 25071 at Preston on a parcels train.

Class 25 loco Nos 25124 and 126 at Preston in the rain.

Class 40 loco No. 40074 at Preston hauling a southbound parcels train.

Class 47 loco No. 47484 *Isambard Kingdom Brunel* at Preston hauling a northbound passenger train.

Class 47 loco No. 47452 at Preston heading south hauling electric loco No. 87027 and its passenger train. This is also one of the earlier photos here, taken when there was no electricity in the overhead wires for some reason, and prior to the 87 loco being named.

Class 83 electric loco No. 83015 at Preston hauling a southbound parcels train.Class 86 electric

Class 86 electric loco No. 86248 at Preston hauling a northbound passenger train.

Class 87 electric loco No. 87002 *Royal Sovereign* at Preston hauling a northbound passenger train.

A pair of Class 40 locos, with No. 40140 leading, powering through Lancaster, a light engine. It appears someone considers 140 to be the *Empress of Tinsley*, if only temporarily.

Class 40 loco No. 40034 *Accra* at Morecambe on 3 September 1982. The loco was parked up on a siding at the side of the station; either it was awaiting duty, or it had failed. Regardless, finding it promenade was a welcome surprise.

Class 47 loco No. 47351 at Hest Bank hauling a northbound freight train of railway lines on 5 August 1982.

*Above*: Class 85 electric loco No. 85036 at Hest Bank hauling a southbound passenger train comprised of an irregular configuration of rolling stock. Taken the same day as the previous photo.

*Left*: Class 47 loco No. 47454 at Carnforth hauling a passenger train from Barrow on 25 August 1982.

Class 40 loco No. 40162 at Carlisle hauling a northbound passenger train. I seem to recall that this was on a Sunday, but I've no idea of the working. It was nice to see this loco with its headcode display intact rather than the domino dots.

Class 47 loco No. 47124 in the southern bay at Carlisle, waiting to depart with the late afternoon passenger train to Newcastle.

Class 87 electric loco No. 87003 *Patriot* arriving at Carlisle with a northbound passenger train.

Class 40 loco No. 40181 at Dumfries hauling a northbound freight train on 7 September 1982.

Class 27 loco No. 27022 at Dumfries hauling a Glasgow to Carlisle passenger train in September 1982.

Class 45 Peak loco No. 45028 at Dumfries hauling a Nottingham to Glasgow passenger train. Taken a year or so earlier than the previous photo.

Class 27 loco No. 27019 at Haymarket station hauling a passenger train into Edinburgh Waverley.

Class 47 loco No. 47707 *Holyrood* at Haymarket hauling a passenger train to Edinburgh. In the early 1980s the Class 27s were cascaded from the Glasgow Queen Street to Edinburgh Waverley push-pull service and replaced by 47/7s. The rolling stock was also upgraded.

HA 08717: Class 08 shunter No. 08717 at Haymarket MPD, Edinburgh.

Class 25 loco No. 25028 at Haymarket MPD.

Class 47 loco No. 47464 at Haymarket MPD.

Class 55 Deltic loco No. 55008 *The Green Howards* at Haymarket MPD.

Class 55 Deltic loco No. 55012 *Crepello* at Haymarket MPD.

Class 40 loco No. 40068 at Kirkcaldy hauling a southbound passenger train.

A pair of Class 20 locos light engine at Motherwell MPD. It was unusual to see two Class 20s running with their cabs together, and although these were only shunting at a shed it was nice to see. The far loco is No. 20027.

Class 27 loco No. 27110 at Motherwell MPD.

Class 37 loco No. 38081 at Motherwell MPD.

Class 20 loco No. 20122 at Glasgow Central on pilot duty.

Class 86 electric loco No. 86218 *Planet* at Glasgow Central waiting to depart with a passenger train.

Class 27 loco No. 27024 at Glasgow Queen Street on pilot duty, with the nose of a Class 47/7 in the immediate foreground. No. 27024 was one of the no-boiler, freight-only locos.

Class 37 loco No. 37012 at Glasgow Queen Street waiting to depart with a late afternoon passenger train.

Class 20 loco No. 20032 at Eastfield MPD, Glasgow.

Class 25 loco No. 25010 at Eastfield MPD.

Class 27 loco No. 27002 at Eastfield MPD.

Class 27 locos at Arrochar and Tarbert hauling north and southbound services on the West Highland Line. These routes were single line with designated passing places. In this photo, the second man of the train to Queen Street has the token ready to hand over. Unfortunately, the station sign hides the number of the loco I was travelling behind to Fort William.

A pair of Class 37 locos with No. 37111 leading at Crianlarich hauling an Oban to Glasgow Queen Street passenger train. The double-heading on this service was apparently a balance working, which possibly occurred on a Friday. A couple of years earlier I had the good fortune to be pulled by a pair of Class 27s on the same service from Crianlarich to Queen Street.

Rendezvous at Rannoch. On a summer evening, Class 27 loco No. 27007 and Class 25 loco No. 25006 cross at Rannoch hauling passenger trains. I was travelling to Glasgow Queen Street on the train being pulled by the 27, whereas the 25 was heading in the opposite direction to Fort William and Mallaig.

Class 37 loco No. 37014 at Fort William MPD. By this time, in May 1982, the Class 37s had displaced the Class 27s on the West Highland Lines.

Class 37 loco No. 37192 leaving Fort William hauling a passenger train to Mallaig.

In the summer of 1978 Class 27 loco No. 27037 approaches Glenfinnan hauling a passenger train from Mallaig to Fort William and Glasgow Queen Street. I was heading to Mallaig, for the first time, on a train hauled by No. 27007. Glenfinnan was the designated passing place.

In May 1982 Class 37 loco No. 37192 approaches Glenfinnan hauling a passenger train from Mallaig to Fort William. On this occasion I was heading to Mallaig on a train hauled by No. 37014.

Class 37 loco No. 37014 at Mallaig waiting to depart to Fort William with a short passenger train of just two carriages.

Class 27 loco No. 27038 arrives at Stirling hauling a passenger train to Dundee.

Class 47 loco No. 47461 at Stirling hauling a southbound passenger train.

Class 20 loco No. 20086 at Perth running light engine.

Three Class 26 locos arriving at Perth hauling a southbound passenger train. Lead loco No. 26019 was detached from the train at Perth. It was purely by chance that I was fortunate enough to be on this platform to capture this triple header arriving.

Class 26 loco No. 26030 at Dundee waiting to depart with a passenger train to Edinburgh. No. 26030 was one of the Inverness-based 26s fitted with double headlights; the others were Nos 15, 22, 32, 35, 38, 39, 41, 42, 43, 45 and 46.

Class 26 loco No. 26044 at Dundee running light engine. Originally 44 was unique in that it was fitted with only a single headlight. Later, other members of the class would be fitted with one headlight, as, in time, were all locos.

Class 47 loco No. 47550 at Aviemore hauling a southbound passenger train that I think is The Clansman.

Class 27 loco No. 27008 at Aberdeen after arriving with a passenger train from Inverness. The loco has had an emergency temporary repair to the front middle window.

Class 26 loco No. 26041 at Elgin hauling an Inverness to Aberdeen passenger train.

Class 26 loco No. 26022 at Inverness. It was rare to see a 26/1 without mini ploughs.

Class 37 loco No. 37157 at Inverness MPD. In due course Class 37s would replace Class 26s hauling passenger trains from Inverness to Kyle, and Wick and Thurso.

Class 26 loco No. 26039 at Inverness arriving with a passenger train from the north. The signal gantry partially hides the train, but I think it has four carriages that would indicate it is the service from Kyle of Lochalsh.

Class 26 loco No. 26042 at Dingwall in the early morning sunshine hauling an Inverness to Kyle of Lochalsh passenger train.

Class 26 loco No. 26034 at Dingwall, hauling an Inverness to Wick and Thurso passenger train, passes loco No. 26035 heading south hauling what appears to be a mixed parcels and freight train.

Class 26 loco No. 26033 arrives at Achnasheen hauling a Kyle of Lochalsh to Inverness passenger train. Although it was spring when I took this photo, there is snow on the distant mountains.

Class 26 loco No. 26042 at Kyle of Lochalsh waiting to depart with a passenger train to Inverness.

Class 26 loco No. 26045 at Rogart hauling an Inverness to Wick and Thurso passenger train. I was travelling on this train and we were held here to allow the train to pass and exchange tokens with the southbound service.

Class 26 loco No. 26041 arrives at Rogart hauling a Wick and Thurso to Inverness passenger train. The second man can be seen dropping off the token, although the remains of the old tablet catcher can be seen on the other side of the loco. The level crossing, the signal box and the semaphore signals add to the interest and lend a timeless quality to the picture.

Class 26 loco No. 26021 arriving at Brora hauling an Inverness to Wick and Thurso passenger train.

Class 26 loco No. 26044 at Brora hauling a Wick and Thurso to Inverness passenger train. I was travelling on this train and we were held here to allow the train to pass the northbound service hauled by No. 26021 in the previous photo.

Class 26 loco No. 26022 at Georgemas Junction. This remote location was where the two portions of the train to and from Thurso and Wick were either separated or put together. The loco that took the portion to Wick was the one that returned south with the train to Inverness. The loco that took the train to or from Thurso was left to its hardship posting.

Class 26 loco No. 26022 waiting to depart with a passenger train to Inverness.